Talkin' to a Man

By, Nandi Eckerson

Talkin' to a Man

Talkin' to a Man

This book is a product of:

Publishing and Marketing Division
and
Sister R.E.I.G.N.

"Don't just exist, when you can Rule Everything In God's Name."

Talkin' to a Man

Talkin' to a Man

 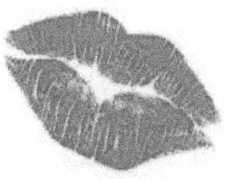 

Talkin' to a Man

Talkin' to a Man

Talkin' to a Man

By, Nandi Eckerson
Anjenco!
Publishing and Marketing Division
Mission, KS

Talkin' to a Man

Copyright 2008 © Anjenco!
Kansas City, KS
66101
All rights reserved. Published in the United States by Anjenco! Except as permitted by copyright law, no part of this publication may be reproduced or distributed in any form or by any means without express permission from the author prior to use.
For information about international copyright relationships, read Circular 38a, *International Copyright Relations of the United States*.
To request permission to reprint any portion of this book, contact Nandi Eckerson at sisterreign@me.com or anjenco@yahoo.com.

All inquiries may be mailed to:

Anjenco!
Publishing and Marketing Division
5400 Johnson Drive #116
Mission, KS 66205

or

Anjenco!
Customer Service Department
P.O. Box 412124
Kansas City, MO 64121

ISBN 978-0-6152-4411-2

Talkin' to a Man

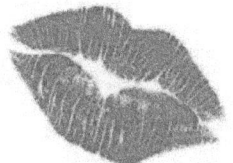  

Talkin' to a Man

Talkin' to a Man

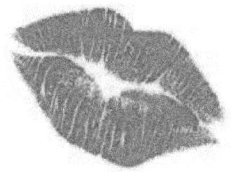  

Talkin' to a Man

Talkin' to a Man

Talkin' to a Man

Talkin' to a Man

Dedication

*I'd like to dedicate this book
to my mother, who taught me that
it's okay to dream, and that loving God
and being intelligent can be
Beautiful.*

Talkin' to a Man

Talkin' to a Man

PREFACE

Some people try to say that men are from Mars and women are from Venus. I just say that people are people and we all have different wants, needs, and thoughts. I will confess some of our desires are the same. I wrote this book to express some of those things and say some things that some women are afraid to say. Don't get me wrong. An increasing amount of us will tell you where to go and how to get there at lightning speed.

Frankly, I love men and I enjoy talking to them too. These poems embody the voice of ladies who have difficulty expressing themselves to men. We listen to the same music. We dance and laugh together. Why do we always talk at each other? We don't get a chance to talk to each other? Can you hear what I'm trying to say?

I hope you enjoy this book of poetry, as much as I enjoyed writing it. And if there's something you don't understand, just turn around and ask a man. I'm sure he's heard it all before.

I like to take the oversight when I write with my creative license.

Nandi Eckerson

Talkin' to a Man

Talkin' to a Man

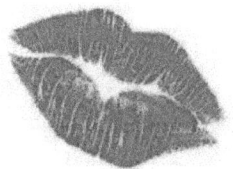  

Talkin' to a Man

Talkin' to a Man

Talkin' to a Man

Talkin' to a Man

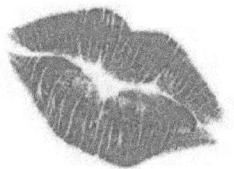  

Talkin' to a Man

Talkin' to a Man

Table of Contents

Dedication	xv
PREFACE	xvii
A Special Aside	xxix
Public Service Announcement	3
Half the Battle	8
Can You Haiku?	18
Don't Assume	24
Got Nothin'	28
Got Poetry?	34
Break of Day	44
Homeless Child	47
Do You Know Who I Am	52
I Am a Writer	54
I Wish	57
I Wish- the Subliminal Version	71
Masterpiece	77
Talkin' to a Man	80

Talkin' to a Man

Table of Contents (continued)

My Enemy	91
Skin Deep	95
My Inspiration	97
Oxymoron	102
Prima Donna	106
Short and Sweet	110
A Problem	113
The Minors	115
What Time Is It?	119
Works Cited	125
About the Author	128

Talkin' to a Man

TALKIN' TO A MAN

TALKIN' TO A MAN

TALKIN' TO A MAN

Talkin' to a Man

Talkin' to a Man

A Special Aside

The italicized words in the first poem presented, is an homage and tribute to the spoken word artist. Each italicized word represents the names of local artists in the Kansas City Metro Area.

I'm just giving a shout out to those on the grind, spitting words from their mind.

Shine, Baby- Baby, Shine!

If that isn't a Public Service Announcement, then I don't know what is.

Kick back. Relax. Don't be afraid to Inhale.

We are going for a ride....
LOL

Talkin' to a Man

Talkin' to a Man

TALKIN' TO A MAN

TALKIN' TO A MAN

TALKIN' TO A MAN

Talkin' to a Man

TALKIN' TO A MAN

TALKIN' TO A MAN

TALKIN' TO A MAN

Talkin' to a Man

PUBLIC SERVICE ANNOUNCEMENT

Ladies and Gentlemen
of the jury I would like to present you
with a *Sistah Solution*.
Keep in mind that the following
conversation is full of *True Speech*.

For those who don't know about
Saving a *Lost Soul* that has lost control
of the rhythm and roll of life,
you may need to engage in some
Visual Therapy with a *Bonafyde G.*

Do you feel me?

Rollin' dice on *Black Ice* is kinda nice
when the *Passion* is right.

Talkin' to a Man

And this certainly is one of the
Best Kept Secrets-- TRUST!!
Believe DUDE.

I wouldn't deceive you.
I'm a sistah like no other,
Not like your sister, your cousin,
or your mother.

Don't get me confused with *Sistah Soulja*.
Don't get it crackin' with all that slappin',
Then turn around and call it love.
Ohh PLEEEZE!!!

You'll need to call a *Priest*
and the police and then pull back a nub.

Talkin' to a Man

OKAY?

But yet again don't get it twisted
I can show you groupie love.
Don't hate congratulate.

I'm just keeping it real-
Sho Nuff.

But I digress,
enough ear pollution,
Let's get back to our *Sistah Solution.*

Ladies there are some things that need
to be left
Unspoken.

Don't trip with the gossip.
I'm not trying to hear it

Talkin' to a Man

This is true *Spoken Knowledge*.

Keep my name out your mouth.
Keep my man out your house.
When you see me, take another route.

This is just between sistahs no doubt.

The aforementioned poem has been a Public Service Announcement.
If there are any questions please call 337-5555.

Did I forget to mention? -
I wanted to thank YOU in advance
for **paying close**
and **careful attention**

Talkin' to a Man

TALKIN' TO A MAN

TALKIN' TO A MAN

TALKIN' TO A MAN

Talkin' to a Man

HALF THE BATTLE

I know you might wonder why
I try to hide from your piercing eyes.

Then I turn around and act a lie,
Like avoiding you is right.

Just know you've done nothing to push
me away.

Deep down in my heart, with you I
want to stay.

Honey, it's not you I am rejecting,
It's just my heart I am protecting.

When you are near my thoughts leave.

Talkin' to a Man

My heart palpitates and my chest heaves.

When I see you, you make me remember how my fleshly temple can shake and tremble.

With the capriciousness
of seven magic O's.
No, I don't mean organisms or Oreos.

These cookies have a need to be set free, by the beat and the tune of a man

who can make me swoon
with those funky cosmic rhythms.

That too is you. You just don't know it yet, Boo.

Talkin' to a Man

Every day, your mind and body I crave.
It's like I'm already your love slave.

Yet we haven't touched or even kissed
And I would be remiss if I didn't mention

The pure bliss I feel in my very soul
when you dock my door, or stand in my dreams.

It's hard to control. I try not to cream
And ruin the innocent image I have created for myself.

So I keep my inner freak remote and stealth, pent up inside.

Isn't that a horrible thing

Talkin' to a Man

to have to hide?

But I can't hide the feelings I have for you- my Neighbor.

I really want to express them with some "Girls Gone Wild Behavior."

So I run and hide keeping it all inside.
Trying not to let you know how I feel.

I even said 'you weren't my man' trying to Tame the sex appeal, but in my mind there is no peace.

At least now I finally realize,
That sometimes a soul has to be baptized

Talkin' to a Man

with the Passion and the fire of the lust that comes with love.

But how can I love you when I don't even know you.

And before this is all said and done,
Let me tell you, I even dreamt of having your son.

And raising your daughters too.
Now do you know why I've been on the run?

I can't stop thinking about you.
Sleepless nights turn into restless days,

I do my best to try and behave.

Talkin' to a Man

"I've got this icebox where my heart used to be.

Boy, I'm really trying to work this out but I'm tired of fighting,

I hope you still want me the way I want you.
I'm really trying to work this out, but I'm tired of hiding.

There's no excuse, no excuse.

I've got this icebox where my heart used to be,

icebox where my heart used to be.

Oh- I'm so cold, I'm so cold, I'm so cold,

Talkin' to a Man

Oh- I'm so cold, I'm so cold, I'm so cold..."

And all I want is for you to keep me warm in your broad tender arms

And make me forget the pain I felt, when I used to be-Reign

And there was a fool named Dominion, who always felt the need to give his dogged opinion.

You are not him and never will be. That's how you've infiltrated my mind with such speed.

I've never had feelings this strong before.

Talkin' to a Man

But when I see your face I only want more of this carnal, brazen, sexy, sassy, lust.

And trust, I'm so hot I could internally combust,

Or have a spontaneous O- then everyone would surely know that you found a way to tap into my inner "nappy headed Ho."

Speaking of "nappy headed Ho's,"
Who'd ever thought
Someone would refer to Don Imus when talking bout
The lust between us.

I may be simpatico,

Talkin' to a Man

but sometimes I am political.

And in all honesty,
I'm a closet freak, not a public ho.

My question for you is how did you know?

"Cuando Quieres, Donde Quieres." I almost lost it then.

But to quote Romeo, when he met Juliet,

"Let me have my sin again."

Darling, I just wanted you to know how I felt,

Talkin' to a Man

Because neither you or nor I are psychic.

I'm so love sick my heart needs help.
I simply can't deny it.

I wanted you to know
my feelings are real.

I want you to feel the way that I feel.

I finally said it.
There you go.

My feelings are at your feet.
Now you know.

And knowing is half the battle.

Talkin' to a Man

Can You Haiku?

======================

Summer breezes blow
Icy raindrops flow at night
Cool nights are so hot.

======================

Jasmine, not a name
Sweet smelling incense, inhale.
Get your fill. Exhale

======================

Talkin' to a Man

Can You Haiku?

======================

Rolling thunder hear
It in the spirit of life
Roll, let it roll now.

======================

Rocky mountain high
Ho the dairy OH!! Climbing
Higher each day. Yo!

======================

Talkin' to a Man

Can You Haiku?

======================

Tiger, Tiggers roar,
Loudly in the darkness.
Will you cry from fear?

======================

Death and Life are one.
Cyclical dancers- Singing.
Overwhelming Time.

======================

Talkin' to a Man

Can You Haiku?

========================

Eternity Calls
The souls of the redeemed
Dastardly no more

========================

Invisible breeze
Passes through our energy
A live connection

========================

Talkin' to a Man

Can You Haiku?

========================

Chair and table meet
Pen and paper glide across
Ballroom dance for minds

========================

Sensual sunrise
Appears in my lover's eyes
Clouds of tears send rain

========================

Talkin' to a Man

Can You Haiku?

========================

Painting paws trick cats
Masterpieces develop
Creeky canvas- sheets.

========================

Trees are flowers. Green
with envy. Challenged by
life's elusive colors.

========================

Talkin' to a Man

DON'T ASSUME

I see you.
You think you know me.

I beg to differ.

Your judgment is swifter
than the salient look
in a young man's eye.

Don't rehearse the verse
or repeat the curse you

Over heard.

I declare the ornate orchestration
of that

Talkin' to a Man

Fixed fabrication that covertly
chose to take

ownership in a fanciful corner
of your mind,

reeks of the pungent
Smell of hypocrisy that

is reminiscent of a pitiful
Porcine boy

that never understands his destiny.

Because he never chose to
evoke the ominous power

of the ancient king's
Prophecy.

Talkin' to a Man

Devastating isn't it?
to know that you too have fallen

Prey to the flamboyant Fallacies
of the supposed fortunate few.

You don't know me,
but I know you.

Don't assume.

Your presuppositions
won't prevail
and
rest assured.

I won't
Fail!

Talkin' to a Man

I know you may think

My seed won't

flower,

Grow

or bloom.

I'll say it again

Please-

Don't assume.

I am more than

YOU know!

Talkin' to a Man

GOT NOTHIN'

What's good for the goose
is good for the gander.

True, true, true-
Did you hear me?

I see you over there.
You looking at me,
Me looking at you.

But it's the same-o,
SAME- O,
you know.

I talked to Terry the other day
playin' on my phone- please.

Talkin' to a Man

I can't understand it.
Last night I was cryin

And Joe wasn't havin it.
Then Terry called
playin on the phone.

I thought I was going
to have a fit.

My sister kept hangin' up the phone.

I wanted you to leave me alone, but
Terry kept playin' in my phone.

Why- WHY?

Now I really started to cry, but Joe
wasn't havin' it.

Talkin' to a Man

He said cryin' wasn't
Going to help nothin'.

He don't know.

I hate to cry in public.

I hate to cry by myself too.

But I can't help but cry
over you.

Now here comes Terry callin' again
Playin' on my phone.

If only God would
come down from heaven
and shut this fool up.

Talkin' to a Man

Joe was right.

It can't be helped.

You can't be helped.

I ain't got nothing left.

I don't have you.
I got nothin'.

Terry is a fool.

I got nothin'.

Joe was right,
although he's too cruel,

Cause you ain't comin' back.

Talkin' to a Man

I got nothing.

Nothin' but

writer's block.

And to me,

that's worse than a heart attack!

Talkin' to a Man

TALKIN' TO A MAN

TALKIN' TO A MAN

TALKIN' TO A MAN

Talkin' to a Man

GOT POETRY?

Got poetry?
Got milk?

It's like rockets
in your pocket,

Cashmere and silk.

Got poetry?
Got cheese?

It's like geekers
wearing sneakers

crying "Baby,
Baby please."

Talkin' to a Man

I got what you want.
I got what you need.

I got the hot poetry

that makes you
want to breathe...

in the fresh cool air,
waiting to exhale.

What the Hell?

Got poetry?

My words can cut
and make you bleed.

Then turn around

Talkin' to a Man

and heal you.

They're better than
the spoken seed.

They get inside to
free the real you.

My words have been planted,
raved, weeded, and saved

in your heart,
in your soul,
in your very mind.

Do you mind?

I need to breathe.
I need to rhyme.

Talkin' to a Man

I am that flagrant piece
you call a dime-

a dime piece.
Yes, a ten.

When I walk down the street,
I control the eyes of men.

Because they knew
that before we ever met.

In this game called life,
I have already won.

You see I always win.

I Got Poetry!

Talkin' to a Man

Not floetry.
Not bigotry.

Not your cousin's
favorite nig- Big Homie.

I have... I got...

The Fierce... the Hot...

Say what you mean,

Flaunt what you got-

Po-e-try.

And don't let me speak
metaphorically.

Talkin' to a Man

PLEAZE!!!!

"Some like it hot,
some sweat
cause
the heat it on."

That's right,
it's on like Donkey Kong.

Don't let me stand in the sand
and get nasty like
Duran Duran.

Awww- Man!!

Got poetry?

Got me?

Talkin' to a Man

No one can be reverent
and content

until

they've had some time well spent
in the

loquacious,
melodic,
erotic,

Tongue twisting,
soul lifting,

Inspiring,
stress relieving Place
that removes pain

Talkin' to a Man

and degradation.
Until you've gone there,

You'll never experience
the heaven sent.
Poetry.

Yes Baby, I mean-
Po-e-try.

I've gone there.

Been there.

I went.

You go.

Talkin' to a Man

See what I mean.
Get it.

Got it?

Good.

Got Poetry?

I knew you would.

Now you can understand.

Everyone from the Hood,
even the man in the Klan,

Presidents and Priests,
And Black Eyed Peas' Will-i-am

Talkin' to a Man

Got Poetry.
It's who you are.

It's who I am.

It's who we be.

Get it.

Got it?

Good.

Got Poetry?

I knew you would.

Talkin' to a Man

BREAK OF DAY

Someone made it a point to say
That the darkest hour is
always before the dawn.

Was it the dawn of mankind
Or that space right before
the dawn of time?

Or maybe it was simply
The period we call-
the BREAKING of day.

My heart is broken anyway.
It can't help it.

It breaks repeatedly

Talkin' to a Man

Every time I think
about you being
Far away from me.

Things seem so dark,
they're just opaque.

What is an hour,
if not an infinity?

I would start to cry,
but that'd seem so fake.

Emotional blackmail.

Is that what they mean?

The darkest hour-
Or is that just something they say

Talkin' to a Man

to make and keep their money green?

Because Lord knows
I'm broke.

This day has broken me.

Talkin' to a Man

HOMELESS CHILD

People are singing about
the "First Noel."
If my mom would let me cuss I'd say
what the Hell....
Does that have to do with me?

We live in a box, ain't

got nothin' to eat.

Momma said that the shelter
would get better.

What does she know?

I just want to forget her...

Talkin' to a Man

but I can't.

She's all I got.

I hate my daddy
for leaving us in this rot.

Kids at school think the
homeless are crazy and dirty.

Not me. I'm balanced.
I got talent. I'm beautiful and flirty.

Teacher got me reading *Romeo and Juliet*. That Mercutio is a fool.

He talkin' 'bout Queen Mab
in that play and cracking jokes.

Talkin' to a Man

It's just another thing all about
rich folks.

But don't err thinkin' I care about
them.

God knows I only have one clean pair of
underwear to fit in.

I'm only keepin' it real.
Know how I feel?

I'm sure you don't
and I hope you won't.

Got people jealous of me
because I'm smart.

But if they knew

Talkin' to a Man

the pain that was in my heart,
maybe it would spark a
change.

Jerk!

Livin' near the mentally deranged
is no piece of cake.

It's a mission and
a vision that Mr. Crusty, the
bumb, wouldn't take.

But don't get it twisted,
I'm the new urban mystic.

In case you didn't know.

With my mind as my landscape,

Talkin' to a Man

I'll be homeless no more.

I live and dwell in a super splinter cell
that's confined to the recesses of my
mind.

Don't judge me.

You may think I'm homeless,
but I'm always at home 'cause I got
peace in my mind and my soul.

This is a day in the life of
a homeless child.

We're all not crazy or stupid
And definitely we're not all wild.

Talkin' to a Man

Do You Know Who I AM?

I am the sunshine. I am the rain. I am sweet tarts and candy canes. I am your peace. I am your love. I am the essence of your being. You cannot live without me. I carry you in my

Talkin' to a Man

heart like a symbiotic twin and that is why I am forever in your mind. I am the sanity that drives you crazy and forces you into my arms. I am the cradle of your innermost clandestine desires.
I am Nandi.

Talkin' to a Man

I AM A WRITER

I evoke moods and movements.

I am a writer, not a poet, but a writer.

Poets dream. They daydream,
They pout. They sigh. They cry.

They write about warm sunny days and sparkling night skies.

I am not a poet who didn't know it.
I don't just write about love and trees,

They write about whispers in the breeze, and corpulent dogs with flees.

Talkin' to a Man

I am a writer, a mad scribe.

I'm a night-typer. You say typist. I say typer. Po-tay-to, po-taw-to.

Yes, misspelling is a risk I take.

Producing thoughts is my aim,
my fatal claim to fame.

As they say, you are what you eat.

I'm a ravenous raven that pilphers
the piteous letters- consonants,

vowels that scream and howl

In the hearts, minds, and
bowels of Mankind.

Talkin' to a Man

I transcend matter, space, and time.

I am a WRITER!!!

Not a player.

Not a fighter,

But a full grown,

bonafide writer.

Talkin' to a Man

I WISH - A Poem in Hi-Def
(not picture in picture but poem in poem)

I wish that I could see your face,
Feel your **touch**, your warm embrace.
Feel your kiss and have just a **taste**
of your love.

I wish.

And as I reminisce about the
fire in your **kiss**,

I dare to care about your hopes,
desires, and your dreams.

And **everything** else in between.

Talkin' to a Man

The feelings I have **can't be erased**,
Though, I'm often pursued... Though,
I'm often chased...

by those who would settle for a sniff,
or even a slight, subtle, faint whiff of
my love.

Let alone a **brazen touch**
followed by a sensuous whine
and a good time that would send **chills**
down a grown man's **spine**.

Better yet, I can **captivate**
a young man's mind.
But I won't even let them close
to **my behind**.
They wish they knew how I was
attracted to you.

Talkin' to a Man

Jealousy will get them nowhere.
They just want to be in your shoes.

They wish. Truthfully, I wish I knew.

I don't **understand** how fate
can cause you to make me **shiver**
from merely having your hand upon my waist?

I do not jest.

You have to do nothing more.
In fact I was swooning
from much less.

I wish I knew.

Don't you?

Talkin' to a Man

I wish the game that
men and women play
didn't exist at all.

To be honest, Honey-
I don't know the rules.
As the song states
"everybody plays the fool."

But how can that be
when my feelings for you
are so true?

Again I wish knew.
I believe that **trust is earned**,
not given freely.

Right now, I would give you everything-
including me.

Talkin' to a Man

That's why I have to work
against myself.

I wish that didn't have to be so,
but you do and say things
that are contradictory.
I guess everyone does, including me.
I wish that were not so.

There are those around
who really know me,
They understand how deep
I would let the desire flow.
They know how far I would
let the love go.

I shield myself and my friends
try to protect me too.

Talkin' to a Man

But do the strong ever really let their
true feelings show?
I don't know. I guess so.
If not, I wish they did.

I hope they do. I do at times. Do you?
To whom? To me? To who?
Being true leaves you open,
susceptible to **emotional pain**.

I wish it were not so, but after the pain-
it's strength we gain.

At least we understand ourselves more.

My heart's been stepped on
once or twice, or even more before.
I don't want it to happen anymore.

Talkin' to a Man

But if it does, I will **regroup**.
My faith will let me recoup and let go of
the dross **from that ill-fated loss.**

Truth is- I've always been faithful.
In relationships, I've always been true.

Who can explain why people
do the things they do?

And even though my last love wasn't,
I pretended I never knew.

And that was something **I vowed**,
if it ever happened again-
that I would never do.

Many odes were written

Talkin' to a Man

to the death of that love, and many more songs are sung about its passing.

I wish I could end all the suffering **and erase senseless heartaches**.

Oh the things we do when we are young, in love, in lust, and dumb...
Since then, **he's apologized**.
I didn't even ask him why.

I never even stopped to cry.
And when he starts to talk about marriage and the throwing of rice,

I don't even begin to think twice about taking him back. I treat him right. I treat him kind,

Talkin' to a Man

But it would be whack to even give him
a chance to get close to my behind.

He had no idea who I am.
He wishes he knew.

There is nothing he can do.
I've let it go and I've moved on.
That situation is through.
My conscious is clear, so what
do I have to fear?

Will you let me give my love to you?
Will your love **be true**?

I wish he would have never showered
me with attention and affection to try to
make up for his deceit and lies.

Talkin' to a Man

He was so distant when
things were fine.
I wish I could've
understood his mind.

Actually, in all honesty **that** is a lie.
Yes, that **is definitely untrue**.
Because if I did- I never would
have opened my eyes
and **my heart** up to you.

You make me want to **trust again**.
I want to be more than your lover.
I want to be your **confidant** and friend.

It **is so profound** how God
can change things around.

I just wish we didn't have to

Talkin' to a Man

take the scenic route and **suffer long**
to figure life's mysteries out.

Also, I'm so glad you
have no time for crazy,
It gives me the opportunity
to remain **a true lady.**

It gives me time to **concentrate**
on how to please a real man.

Of course all real men **love Christ**.
At least they do when they figure out
His way is right.

I wish everyone could see the light.

And I hope tonight, you begin to
understand what I want in my man.

Talkin' to a Man

I will try to be clearer in my words and my thoughts.

That's **not always easy** for me because there are a few **emotional battles** lying around out there that I have had to fight.

I won, but when the fighting was done, my desire was only for joy and fun.

After the rush, I thought the emotional wounds were too much.

I wish I never had to **go through them.**
I wish I never knew them.
But it's because of them,
that I **have wisdom.**

Talkin' to a Man

Struggle and chaos can
produce some beautiful results.

Maybe that's why **I can feel you.**
I won't leave you,
unless you want me to.

As you say- "I got you."
Daddy, I hope you know
you got me too.

Maybe one day we'll
"make it do, what it do."

I wish the things you do to me are
the very same things I do to you.

I wish.

Talkin' to a Man

TALKIN' TO A MAN

TALKIN' TO A MAN

TALKIN' TO A MAN

Talkin' to a Man

I Wish- the Subliminal Version

I wish –
touch
Taste,

kiss,
everything

can't be
erased,

brazen touch,

chills
down
spine,

Talkin' to a Man

captivate
my behind.

understand

shiver

I wish...

I don't know the rules.

"everybody plays the fool."

trust is earned,
- including me.

I wish

understand

Talkin' to a Man

I shield
true feelings

emotional pain.
- it's strength

regroup,
from that ill-fated loss.

Truth is-

I vowed,
and erase senseless heartaches.

he's apologized.

He wishes he knew.

Talkin' to a Man

My conscious is clear,

do I have to fear?

be true

things were fine.

that
is definitely untrue.

would
my heart
trust again?

confidant

so profound

Talkin' to a Man

take the scenic route

suffer long.

have no time for crazy,
a true lady,

concentrate

love Christ.

His way is right.

understand.

That's not always easy
- emotional battles.

go through them.

Talkin' to a Man

have wisdom.

Struggle

produce some beautiful results.

I can feel you.

you got me too.

the very same.

I wish.

Talkin' to a Man

MASTERPIECE

Candles in the night
Illuminate paintings

On the walls of my
Antiquated museum

See the flicker
Feel the warmth
See the flame

As it dances across
a Monet, a Picasso.
A Van Gogh, a Matisse.

Not just romantic
It's wonderfully spastic.   **Masterpiece.**

Talkin' to a Man

TALKIN' TO A MAN

TALKIN' TO A MAN

TALKIN' TO A MAN

Talkin' to a Man

TALKIN' TO A MAN

TALKIN' TO A MAN

TALKIN' TO A MAN

Talkin' to a Man

TALKIN' TO A MAN

Balance the equilibrium
of this requiem,
of this poem.

What is it about?

You have a right to ask.
Using your mind this time
is your task.

Figure it out.

I'm not talking to myself.

You poke and jab at my heart
and stab at my mind

Talkin' to a Man

trying to find out
why I wrote this.

It's not about love,
but it's about a kiss,
A Kiss with a twist.

Call it the credible tool
That will make wise a fool.

"Are you sure about that?"

Yes as serious as a heart attack.

It's an aphrodisiac
that will make you fall in love,
if you're not still caught up in lust.

"You mean it's enticing and intriguing."

Talkin' to a Man

Absolutely and it's pleasing.

I would not err,
nor do I care about
what others think of me.

Although it may be
a challenge to be me,
to be who I am.

That is the story of every
Revolutionary.

So, I'll just grin and bare it.

You can't make me stop or quit.

I'd like to think that I'm
the next Angela Davis,

Talkin' to a Man

Condeleeza, or even Ruby Dee.

But you can't handle that.

Are you sure within yourself?
Secure and self-assured?

Because the other day
You made me wonder
And question my
Strength and ability.

And baby that's not me.
Why did I write this?

I'm just talkin' to a man.

Talkin' to YOU- man.
Because you ARE a man

Talkin' to a Man

who needs to know that
I'm balanced.

Please!! I have class,
I have a brain.

I'm not just boobs
and a tasty piece of ass.

I don't chase men down
or spread myself around.

I'm not a little girl, a whore, or fast.
Being smart IS pretty.
Being black is TOO.

Having a degree is an asset.
Why have one when
you can have two?

Talkin' to a Man

I'm so smooth, I don't even
Hang it over your head,
The big one or the little one,

Isn't that what you were looking for?

I've got a good head on my shoulders..

You should like it,
And love it,
and think more of it.
I'm more than any bubble headed,
bobble head,
bimbo, or skank.

I'm not a gold digger.
I have my own money
in the bank.
Excuse me banks.

Talkin' to a Man

I have more than just one.
In case you want to know.

Why should that scare you?
Are you a coward?

My job is to complete you,
Not to compete with you.

My behind might be an asset,
But my mind is too.

Booty and beauty fades.
They sag and decrease with age.

What are you looking for-
a foolish empty headed whore
who doesn't know how
to take care of house and home?

Talkin' to a Man

I want it all and can have it too.

And I want to make it happen with you.

Remember that jingle for Enjoli?
"I can bring home the bacon,
fry it up in a pan,
and never let you forget
you're a man."

Now I'm showing my age,

But you ought to want a woman
who can cook, pray, sew,
work, and clean.

Because if not-
You'll surely know
frustration's rage.

Talkin' to a Man

Remember Bill
with his trophy wife,
Miss Teen Queen.
They got divorced
after two years
because he was tired
of being dirty and lean.

Children were out of
THE question.
She was trying to stay thin.

Well, that is the downfall
of some of you poor men.

Being a size ten,
should make me a ten.
At least you won't starve.

Talkin' to a Man

And you won't have to
worry about me
spending every dime we have
or running up the
credit cards.

I'm a grown woman,

A real woman,

A know just how
you feel woman,

and if that's something
you can stand-

Let me know if I'm talkin'
To a REAL man.
Holla!

Talkin' to a Man

TALKIN' TO A MAN

TALKIN' TO A MAN

TALKIN' TO A MAN

Talkin' to a Man

My Enemy

Tell me, tell me friend where the friendship ends and
where love begins.

I told you that I love you like a brother,

Somehow over the years you are now closer to me than my own mother.

I'm confused.

I'm confused at how our friendship abused these emotions.

It took them hostage and infused the

Talkin' to a Man

torrent of the torment of this feeling
that I have inside.

It's majestic.

The way these carefree feelings
have emancipated the caustic
constipated nature that one finds
in an intuitive intellectual mind.

So answer me before I become
even more perturbed.
Now isn't that absurd?

How can the calm, cool, and
collected maneuver in the atrocity of
what others can't see this mist,
this haze, this Emotion between you
and me.

Talkin' to a Man

It's hellacious, if not salacious.

How could I let this be?

Regal royalty having been set free
from the lifeless shell of my own self
imposed death knell.

For whom does the bell toll?
Do you know?

Friend of mine,
enemy too why do I do
what you do the hoodoo of this voodoo-
Déjà vu Boo.

Well friend it would be fair
to say that's all's fair in
love, as well as, in war.

Talkin' to a Man

If this love is to last-
we can be friends no more.

So tell me,
tell me what is this friction
between us?

What shall it be?

Are you my friend
or my enemy?

Talkin' to a Man

Skin Deep

Beauty penetrates deeper than that layer called the skin. The Beauty that I am seeking is far greater than mere men. It goes past the swerves of sensual curves. Why just creep, play around and sleep with strangers and

Talkin' to a Man

have my heart, mind, body and soul in danger- all because I fell in love with the epidermal layer. Who's getting played and who's the player? Now how thick or thin is your skin? Think about it. That's deep.

-From a MAN

Talkin' to a Man

MY INSPIRATION

My mother, my brother, my sister,
My cousin- the little boy down the
street
That plays the dozens.

These are the folks who inspire me,
Because without them, there would be
no me.
For whatever reason
I believe it's an act of treason to forget
Where we come from.

Folks do it all the time.

Do you expect me to pay you,
To do you, while you do me?

Talkin' to a Man

You can fake the funk while you front
And forget where I come from?

No my name ain't Amos
And one day I will be famous.
And for that reason I won't forget
The dedicated teachers and true preachers
Who taught me to work hard
And to never forget to reverence God.

I'll remember
The folks in the hood
who said it was all good
to be honest and fight
to get out of the projects.

They told me to go to college
so I could be a social reject.

Talkin' to a Man

Their words of wisdom inspired
And my soul they protect.

I will always remember
And never forget.

I can't forget my boy
Round the way, who married that girl
Who laid up and had his Bay-bay
'Cuz he wanted his family to stay together.

What the heck?

Be separated for a stinky welfare check?

He works two jobs, she works one.

Talkin' to a Man

And in December, she's gonna have a son.

Stay together?
They go to church and pray together.
Why be a crippled welfare patient?
He said fix the cause
Fix the nation.

The recipients are sick
And you got to be quick
To find social salvation.

Now that's inspiration.

So to those of you who asked me to speak
And wanted to know why
I don't glorify super freaks.

Talkin' to a Man

I hate it when scum goes platinum,
And the children and the DJ's say
"Well there ain't nothing else to play."

As long as God is in heaven above
I'm gonna show my people love.

If for no other reason,
it's because no one else does.

That is my inspiration.

My God, my people, my love.

PEACE.

Talkin' to a Man

OXYMORON

Do you want to play a game?
Say my name, say my name....
No, it's not what you think.

I am at the brink of the place where we learn,
the place of discovery the place of no return.

Before I forget, let's play a game
I'll be the Devil' Advocate.

I'm not saying that I'm trying
To mess with your mind,
But you know what I do.
Don't you?

Talkin' to a Man

My mamma didn't raise no fool.
What about you?
Do you remember on that date
When I bought some cupcakes
And your little cousin called me fake.

You know what I'm talking about.
And you told me that the taste
Of my sugar honey dipped sweetness
was a big mistake.

That was when the eye of recognition
kicked in
To overdrive and reverse.

Honey, it was a blessed curse.
I looked at you and I realized
That our connection rippled like the
mere detection

Talkin' to a Man

of
A fatal attraction that was a distraction
From the direction I was headed in.

I was in total defection of my singleness
In mind because I was caught up in
Your ying-yang, yo-yo bang,
Shallow-deep pit of clamorous- peace
And I'm not havin' it.

Not anymore. So who is the moron
And who is the phenomenon?
Now that's an oxymoron.

Oh and if I'm so fake,
Then how can I keep it so real?
Feel me?

Talkin' to a Man

TALKIN' TO A MAN

TALKIN' TO A MAN

TALKIN' TO A MAN

Talkin' to a Man

PRIMA DONNA

Do you wanna Prima Donna?

Do you want one?
Do you got one?
Can you be one?
Can you see one?

Me? I'm a free one, footloose and fancy.

That is who I am,
that is who I be.

In case you didn't know, I have dollars
I have dough. So when you see me

You know you wanna be me

Talkin' to a Man

but you can't even see me.

You can't see the true me,
not my real identity.

Do you wanna prima donna
In full sophistication, with
Rest and relaxation in your
Heart and soul?

Do you wanna
Know the Prima Donna's soul?

I'm too hot to handle, too cold to hold.

A Prima Donna's fresh,
a Prima Donna's bold.

Not an idiot savant

Talkin' to a Man

full of want
professing to know something,
full of vain glory.

You- fool, don't know the whole story
You don't know nothing
To say the least.

Just Peace,

adios,

kick rocks,

Vaya con Dios.

Why?

Because your toes

Talkin' to a Man

I'll roast in the sands of time.

I spit the most sincere rhyme
That can blow the average mind.

So do you wanna Prima Donna?

Can you get with this,
my state of bliss?

Or is it a mild tryst down memory lane
That you proclaim to be your claim to fame.
So do you wanna Prima Donna?

Do you Wanna Prima Donna?

Do you WANNA PRIMA DONNA?

Talkin' to a Man

SHORT AND SWEET

Hey You!
Got any ideas?

Keep it to the point.
Make it short and sweet.

Keep your rap tight
And maybe we could meet.

And talk about the real things,
the chill things, the way you
make me feel things.

Because
ignorance is not bliss, and your
conversation is hit or miss,

Talkin' to a Man

neither here nor there,
when you talk to me.

Talk about being

somewhere,

something,

somebody.

So please-

Keep it
short and sweet.
Got any
Ideas?

Talkin' to a Man

TALKIN' TO A MAN

TALKIN' TO A MAN

TALKIN' TO A MAN

Talkin' to a Man

A PROBLEM

Don't wallow in it.
Just swallow it.

Your pride-
I mean.

Let your sorrow
Reappear tomorrow.

Live for the now.
Don't ask how.

Always lend,
Don't borrow.

Don't wallow in it.

Talkin' to a Man

Turn it around.
Spin it.

Even though
your joy is hallow,
your heart is sallow,

you know for certain
you're not shallow.

So when Mr. Problem
Extends his hand

To shake yours

and says "Hello."

Bid him "Adieu"
And go.

Talkin' to a Man

THE MINORS

Your level of expertise
is nothing to be messed with.
If blessings were a curse,
Then I'd say you've been blessed with
Being a minor, college major,
working in the fields
Of corporate "wanna be" labor.
You don't even have a real job.

Somebody tried to tell me,
that you went to Howard.
You're not even smart enough
to get into that Ivory Tower.

You major in the minors,
You're a whiner, or better yet a wiener.

Talkin' to a Man

Yellow streaked coward
Thinking you're a fashion model,
You do don't look like Terrance
Howard.
Have nothin', know nothin', want
nothin'- fool.

That's right! I said it!

Don't look at me like that.

Don't cut me off .
If we're going to have an argument,
Let me get it out.
You're the one
who believed that he said,
she said, I said, you said,
that he did, what she did,
when I did, what you did.

Talkin' to a Man

But we didn't do that.
GOSSIP is a trip.

More people are meaner by the minute,
Following the minors,
Then turning around to spin it.
Yes- spit it.
Minor information twisters,
I am waiting for their tongues to blister.
Why won't people quit it?

If you want to know just ask me.
Oh my goodness.
Oh my God.
Just ask me before you try to laud
And lord your opinions over me,
Under me, around me,
Here me? Heard me? Sound me?

Talkin' to a Man

But whatever you do,
Could you please not hound me?
Put those pitiful, petty, picayune, pissant,
Puddle swallowing people in the past.
Small minds think the minors are sublime.
GOSSIP is a trip.

Side with them or side with me.
Be a Major Minor if you want to be.
I, my friend am powerful beyond belief.

I'm loving it too.

If I were you, I'd make a change.
Listening to phony lies
Is just so deranged.

Talkin' to a Man

WHAT TIME IS IT?

What time is it?
Time?
Haven't you heard the saying or the
rhyme about
time?

About the stitch in time that saves
nine.
Or that other thing – You know
It's a cinch by the inch,
But it's hard by the yard?
(What is a cinch anyway?
Isn't that something you order for
dessert at a French
restaurant?

Talkin' to a Man

"I'll have the Cinch Ala' Rang' with my soufflé.")

I don't know who they were talking to,
A cinch.
But they sure weren't talking to you.
We talked for one minute and I was confused.
I asked you for an answer to my question
And you flat out refused.

Do your sins behind closed doors
Quote the Raven never more,

turn out the light thinking nobody knows.
Quote the Raven never more.

Talkin' to a Man

One of these mornings your sins will find you out.

Oh my God, won't that be a bore?
Quote the Raven never more.

Poe- you know.

But I digress.

I tell the truth and do not jest.
Wasn't this rhyme supposed to be about time?

What time is it?
You heard me ask the question.
Will you signify?
You can tell the truth or just tell a lie.
(That's what you do anyway.)

Talkin' to a Man

I'm not trying to trick you.
That sure wouldn't benefit me.
My mama didn't raise no fool.
Please!!!
I'm just trying to get to the truth.
THE TRUTH!
Can't you see?

What time is it?
Can you see?
Can't you see what people are doing?
What does it all mean?
Can you tell me?
I don't know.

What time is it?
Is it time to be a hero?
Or is it time to play the fool?
The only person who can tell me is you.

Talkin' to a Man

But NO- you're blind to the entire thing.
I don't have time for that.

What time is it anyway?
You are a satiable brick wall.
I don't have time to play games.
Time? Tii-imme!
What time is IT?

9 o'clock? Oh.
Well-
Thank you very much.
That's all I needed to know.

Talkin' to a Man

TALKIN' TO A MAN

TALKIN' TO A MAN

TALKIN' TO A MAN

Talkin' to a Man

Works Cited

Omarion, "Ice Box," from 21 (Columbia Records, c2006) CD

Arcadia, "Some Like It Hot," from So Red the Rose (Capitol Records, c1985) CD

Poe, Edgar Allen. "The Raven," New York Evening Mirror. 29 January 1845

Talkin' to a Man

TALKIN' TO A MAN

TALKIN' TO A MAN

TALKIN' TO A MAN

Talkin' to a Man

TALKIN' TO A MAN

TALKIN' TO A MAN

TALKIN' TO A MAN

This book is a product of:

Publishing and Marketing Division
5400 Johnson Drive #116
Mission, KS 66205

Customer Service Department
P.O. Box 412124
Kansas City, MO 64121

AND

"Don't just exist, when you can
Rule Everything In God's Name."

www.sisterreign.com

Talkin' to a Man

About the Author

Nandi Eckerson is an educator and insightful author who is an observer of human behaviors. She gives voice to both relationship and women's issues. Nandi Eckerson has also authored the book Miracles Called Cornbread, an expression of urban culture and a reflection of the human soul.

www.ingramcontent.com/pod-product-compliance
Lightning Source LLC
Chambersburg PA
CBHW030936090426
42737CB00007B/452